Forest Fires

Run for Your Life!

by Josephine Nobisso

For information contact: MONDO Publishing, 980 Avenue of Americas, New York, NY 10018
Visit our web site at http://www.mondopub.com

Printed in the United States of America
02 03 04 05 06   9 8 7 6 5 4 3 2

Book Designed by Jean Cohn
Cover composition by Steven Umansky
ISBN: 1-57255-793-1

Library of Congress Cataloging-in-Publication Data

Nobisso, Josephine.
    Forest Fires : run for your life! / by Josephine Nobisso.
        p. cm.
    Summary: Discusses three major forest fires in the United States and Canada, including
events leading up to them, how they were fought, and their aftereffects
    ISBN 1-57255-793-1
    1. Forest fires--Juvenile literature. 2. Forest fires--United States--Juvenile literature. 3.
Forest fires--Ontario--Juvenile literature. [1. Forest fires.] I. Title.

SD421.23 .N63 2000
363.37'9--dc21
                                                        00-021620

For Jimmy Colaneri, "Lighthorse,"
my teacher and friend

—J. N.

Contents

CHAPTER ONE:

Fire in Yellowstone National Park
~1~

CHAPTER TWO:

The Hinckley Fire of Minnesota
~16~

CHAPTER THREE:

The Matheson Fire in Ontario, Canada
~25~

CHAPTER FOUR:

Nature Gets the Last Word
~34~

INDEX
~39~

Fire in Yellowstone National Park

In the Summer Forest

In the middle of a summer forest, bomber planes swoop above the treetops. Dozens of bulldozers slam into the growth, leveling everything in their paths. Helicopters buzz, dropping men, women, and supplies.

These people are not fighting a war. They are a small part of a huge and frantic "army" struggling to save the forest. They are firefighters.

An airplane, acting as a fire extinguisher, drops fire retardant to blanket a burning area.

Miles and miles of Yellowstone National Park and the woods around it are in flames. All park visitors have been *evacuated*, told to leave. All the people in the surrounding communities are on alert. The deer, bison, elk, and bear who have not already left keep a watchful eye.

How It Started

The fire has its beginning on a hot summer night in 1988. It hasn't rained in weeks. Thunder comes, rumbling like an empty stomach hungry for a storm. The forest floor is piled ankle deep with dry leaves and brittle pine needles. It is littered with dead branches and twigs. The leaves of the lower bushes have turned a dusty gray. The

How Are Fires Fought?

Most forest fires in North America are put out by professional firefighters using hand tools such as rakes and axes. Their most complicated aids are gas saws and backpack water pumps. For fires that get too big, however, they must use remote control television, detailed photography, heat-sensing devices, aircraft, radar, and even satellite.

Yellowstone National Park in flames

Nature, in the form of lightning from the skies, often strikes the "matches" that will ignite the land.

grasses in the forest meadows look more blond than green.

On this night, dry lightning stamps jagged wounds on the sky, but, still, the air does not smell of rain. Thunder rolls again and again, with deafening cracks. Lightning pulses across the night, zapping the woods like lit matches.

How Many Types of Forest Fires Are There?

The United States and Canadian Forest Services divide fires into three categories:

1 **Surface fires** *burn grasses, bushes, and debris on the forest floor before they climb their way up trees. These are the most common and easiest to fight.*

2 **Crown fires** *advance from treetop to treetop, and burn independently of surface fires. These are the fastest spreading.*

3 **Ground fires** *progress slowly, smoldering under the litter on the forest floor. The least spectacular, these fires are the hardest to control.*

Should We Let It Burn?

Rangers in their lookout stations see flames flaring up. Here! There! Dozens of spots throughout the forest catch fire.

Since the fires are in the wild areas of the big park, and are not threatening people or buildings, the park managers don't call in the firefighters. The rangers know that most forest fires go out by themselves, burning away only very small patches

Surface fire

2

of the vast woods. They also know something most people find hard to believe: some years there are 72,000 forest fires in the United States.

Fire Is Natural to Forests

Forest rangers also know that nature uses fires to tend its forests. Fire clears out the fallen-away debris of the woods. It takes down weak trees, creating meadows of fresh growth that will eventually become groves of new trees.

Some trees, like the *lodgepole pine*, are ready to confront fires even as they grow. Besides its regular cones, the lodgepole produces others that are "glued" shut with *resin*. It is only after a fire, when this resin has melted, that seeds are released to start new trees.

Burned lodgepole pinecone with sapling sprouting up from one of its seeds

Fire Protects the Forest

The rangers know that fires create their own kind of protection against future fires. Forest fires tend to burn in an open-

Most wildfires leave some old growth untouched. The areas they do scorch will be open to new growth.

hand pattern, leaving wide patches untouched between the burned "fingers." Those burned fingers may not catch fire again for hundreds of years.

A fire climbed only partway up this hill, creating diversity there.

Deer Need Grass

Deer live in the deep woods, but they need grass to eat. If a forest doesn't have meadows, deer come to the edge of the woods to graze. This is why we see them feeding on the sides of roads.

If parts of the woods are burned once in a while, the whole forest stays healthy because diversity is created. When many kinds of vegetation grow, the forest stays strong. Trees of different varieties and differing heights can catch the sunlight. Many kinds of animals can make their homes there.

But, if a forest gets to be all one age, all its trees get old or diseased at once. The same kinds of animals tend to live there, struggling over limited food. The weak trees can catch fire at the same time.

Teams study the courses of Yellowstone's fires before deciding on a plan for controlling them.

Keeping Track

Even though the rangers decide not to fight the fires yet, they watch the flare-ups carefully. They name them. They follow their courses, marking their progress on maps. If the fires meet up and create a big fire, that can mean big trouble.

One Hundred Years of Putting out the Flames

For 16 years, the Yellowstone rangers have been letting the forest fires run their own courses, as long as they weren't threatening people or private property. The fires of this electric, rainless night in 1988 look like any others. Even the forest animals are moving calmly away from the smoke and flame. They have plenty of time to get out of the fires' reaches.

Before this, for almost one hundred years, the United States Forest Service had controlled almost all fires. The Canadian Forest Service, too, had put theirs out for almost as long. The United States began this cautious program because of the most devastating fire in its history, "The Great Hinckley Fire," in Minnesota, in the year 1894. The Canadians started theirs some years after being shocked by an unusual fire in Matheson, Ontario, in 1916.

Animals graze and drink calmly as a fire burns in their forest.

By 1988, generations of firefighters have been doing such a good job of putting out flare-ups that, in Yellowstone, enormous amounts of kindling are ready to burn. Many of the standing trees are weak and full of insects. The whole forest is tired.

A ground crew heads out to control a fire.

Ready for a "Burn"

Since the winters in Yellowstone are long and severe, and the summers short and rainy, people have thought that a really big forest fire could not be lit in Yellowstone even if someone tried.

But by 1988, as the rangers look back over 112 years of weather records for Yellowstone National Park, they see that it is having its driest season. The creeks are running slowly. Lakes are shrinking.

Winds, as fast as speeding cars on highways, begin whipping up the small, usual fires, adding to the winds which all fires make on their own. These hot winds are toasting up the forest, making it ready for a big "burn."

Crowning

Suddenly, from the fires started by lightning and one small man-made fire deep in the forest, trees begin igniting into swirls of flames. They explode, sounding like firecrackers ringing out in the night.

Firebrands, chunks of burning wood the size of apple pies, blow apart from the trees. They fly hundreds of feet and then burst apart like fireworks, sending lit darts streaking through the air to ignite everything they spear. The tops of trees begin to *crown*, or catch fire, even before the underbrush burns!

A flame, whipping in the fire winds, wraps itself around the trunk of a tree.

Flames and gases shoot high above the fire, superheating the air and crowning into the trees.

"Call in the Hot Shots!"

The park managers rush to put out calls for help. Thousands of firefighters begin streaming in to fight the hundreds of Yellowstone blazes. Experienced *Hotshot* teams come. These men and women are the most highly trained of all the fighters. Camps are set up all over the vast park so that the firefighters can sleep and eat close to their battles.

Members of a ground crew, outfitted in lightweight, fire-resistant clothing, lug a hose toward the Yellowstone blazes.

The Fight Begins

The thousands of workers fight with shovels, digging up dirt to smother the burning bushes and smoldering grasses. Throughout the forest, teams hook up pumps to the streams and ponds, making water gush from miles of hose. They put out some flames, but new ones keep spurting up.

With their chain saws, the teams cut trees so that they fall toward the fires. With their bulldozers, they scoop up debris and shove it to either side, carving wide, bare paths, or *fire lines* on the forest floor. When the fire reaches the strip of bare mineral dirt, the firefighters expect it to run out of fuel and die down.

A firefighting team sometimes works very close together to be sure they've extinguished every spark.

How Hot Is Hot?

In most forest fires, more is destroyed by heat than is consumed by fire. If exposed for an hour to 120°F (49°C), the tissue under the tree bark, phloem and cambium, is killed, even if the tree remains standing. Death to the same tissue will come instantly if exposed to 147°F (64°C). Woody material, however, will not ignite until the temperature reaches a whopping 650°F (343°C), with a flame temperature of 1600 to 1800°F (870–980°C)!

Standing in the middle of a newly cut fire line, this unmasked firefighter surveys the dying sputters of a blaze he helped control.

Fighting Fire with Fire

The firefighters also rush to create *backburn*, deliberately setting fires from safe places like the man-made fire lines and roads or the natural rivers and streams. Backburn fires move along swiftly to meet the main blaze the firefighters are trying to stop. By the time the two fires join, both have used up all the fuel in that section of the forest, and then both have to die down. Everything beyond the fire line is usually saved.

Firefighters ignite a "prescribed burn," torching the vegetation along a river which will become a "fire line," the place where a fire dies down.

To start the backburn, the firefighters run through the forest, setting fire after fire with chemical torches. They drop explosive "bombs" the size of Ping-Pong balls from helicopters. They shoot flaming flares into the deep woods.

Surprised

The Forest Service has controlled many fires in this way, working with nature to let fire take its course while keeping it from running wild. But this fire of 1988 is proving to be very different. Even the experienced Hot Shots see things they've never seen before. Not depending only on the ground debris for fuel, this fire is jumping the fire lines because it is burning in the tree-tops first.

Sometimes the best way to stop an advancing fire is to burn up fresh vegetation before the flames can feed on it.

Fire winds twist like hot cyclones, sucking up and igniting everything in their paths. They snap trunks the width of men's waists. They uproot trees, piling the remains like charred pickup sticks.

Clouds of smoke towering over mountains will spread over hundreds of miles, dropping black "rain" onto distant places.

The heat becomes so intense it even splits stone boulders. The combination of drought and wind in an old forest full of debris has turned a normal forest fire into a *firestorm*.

Firestorms

A firestorm is a rare phenomenon. With drought, dry air, strong winds, high temperatures, and plenty of woody fuel, a regular forest fire can burn so hot that it creates its own cyclone-like storm system. Regular forest fires move along at up to 10 miles per hour, but firestorms travel at the speed of hurricanes.

This fire is burning so hot, it is out of human control.

A Flurry of Slurry

The firefighters call in low-flying airplanes to drop wet chemicals that blanket the forest with a coat of "paint" called *slurry*. These chemicals, a mixture of fertilizer and water, are dyed red for visibility. As the hatches open, the slurry looks like huge, exotic red flowers blooming midair.

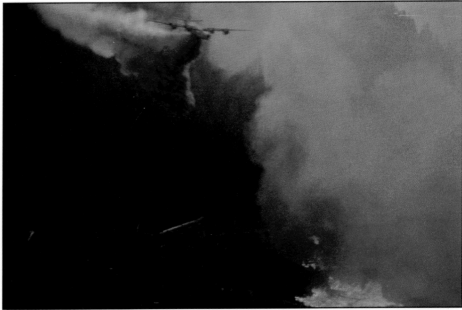

Fire coughs up black smoke as a fighter plane splashes it with wet slurry.

Roaring, licking, spitting, and crackling, fire feeds itself on the feast of forest fuel.

Sights and Sounds

With bloodshot eyes that smart and tear, the men and women on the ground peer up into the smoke whenever they hear a roar like aircraft. They hope for more slurry, but often, the noise is created by winds through the forest, like a thousand jets.

A confusion of sounds rings the firefighters. Lower vegetation burns instantly to ashes, letting out soft hisses as they collapse. Flaming trees splinter as they hit the forest floor. The burning pine needles whistle like mad tea kettles. Billions of heated seeds pop as if from popcorn-makers out of control. To hear one another speak on their portable telephones and radios, the firefighters shout. To communicate on the ground, they scream.

Helicopters buzz above, heading for isolated spots that cannot be reached by the most rugged vehicles, or even by mule. *Smoke jumpers* leap out of helicopters, parachuting down to fight more and more small fires before they can spread.

With many of the water sources dried up by drought, some helicopters must travel distances to find water and bring it to the fire.

Air and Ground Attack

The slurry planes return again and again, sweeping low. Their electronic heat scanners make living maps of the fires below. From an opening built to drop wartime bombs, each plane lets fall 2,000 gallons of slurry, thick like heavy cream. They aim just ahead of the fire, to *retard*, or slow, its progress.

Helicopters outfitted with buckets scoop water from ponds. When their aim is on target, splashing onto the heart of the worst blazes, the crews let out cheers while the forest spits up billowing clouds of black smoke.

A "bomber" flies dangerously low, splashing a high concentration of slurry onto a targeted blaze.

In this way, firefighters are able to get closer to the center of the fires, to bring in machines and tools. One blaze after another is being brought under control. Doing this enough might put out all the fires in the whole forest.

Month After Month After Month

No one guesses when the firefighting first begins that Yellowstone will burn for three months. But the fire advances, gobbling up forests in three states. Its debris blocks the sun so that parts of North America are covered in its "fog." Black "rain" falls on ships five hundred miles out to sea. Firefighters come, fight, leave, and return, relieving others who will do the same.

Over one million acres are involved in the Yellowstone fires, and 440,000 of them get completely burned. When it is all over, the firefighters are relieved to announce that not one human life has been lost.

The Aftermath

From the air, flyers see that the park looks like a huge green blanket with black holes burned into it. The fire zigzagged, making a jigsaw puzzle pattern of young, middle-aged, and old growth. Nature has left different habitats for animals and plants. Nature has left diversity.

The winter sun filters in through a burned-up, quiet forest.

The Burning Question

Today, advanced equipment is used to detect and fight fires. Satellites in space beam important information to Earth. This helps the Forest Service decide what to do about each fire. *To*

Fire has left a "crazy quilt" of charred patches alongsde the colorful ones.

let it burn or not to let it burn—that is the question. Call in the "troops," or let nature be its own caretaker? Everything must be considered: weather and forest conditions, danger to lives and property.

Before the Technology

The technology that helps forest rangers today was not always there, of course. It started in the United States because of that Great Hinckley Fire of 1894, and in Canada, after the Matheson Fire during World War I, in 1916.

CHAPTER TWO

The Hinckley Fire of Minnesota

The Great Fire in Minnesota

We have the newspaper reports of the Hinckley Fire, and we have amazing eyewitness accounts. Each one of the thousands of survivors had a moving story to tell.

Hinckley, before the fire

To take a look at The Great Hinckley Fire, we have to go back in time to a scorching summer day in 1894. It is the period of history called "The Industrial Revolution." Minnesota is a busy place. Factories buzz in the towns. In the woods, people have set up logging camps and stone quarries. Immigrant settlers are building homes. Steam locomotives chug along several railway lines. Traveling salesmen pack their bags onto the system of rails or load up wagons to trundle over dirt roads. Adventure-seekers come and go, hiking through the towns, taking odd jobs. The roofs of churches and synagogues rise up from the bustling streets.

The lumberjacks have declared 1894 a drought year. Fires have been burning for a month now, but these are common in the Minnesota woods. Everyone is used to having the air smoky during hot weather.

Before 1894, the Eastern Hotel in Hinckley served a steady flow of travelers.

It's Harvest Time

On September 1, people are harvesting their crops for the winter. They cut long hay grasses that will feed their farm animals during the cold months.

Two young men, Peter Nyberg and Gus Johnson, leave their settlement, Mission Creek, to go haying. They plan to stay in the wilderness overnight. The air in their little town is foggy from the smoke of a distant fire, but no one pays much attention.

Peter and Gus travel deep into the woods, looking for good meadows. A sudden rush of flames appears out of the forest. Taller than the tallest building they can imagine, it rolls toward them like an ocean wave tumbling toward the shore.

The young men jump into a stream to dunk themselves. The fire passes. They look around. All the hay has been burned. They spend the rest of the day exploring, unaware of what is about to happen in the town they've left behind and in all of eastern Minnesota. That night they sleep in a section of unburned woods.

All the Earth Looked Dipped in Blood

North of them, up in nearby Sandstone, Emil Anderson, the handsome young pastor of the Swedish Congregational Church,

Emil Anderson

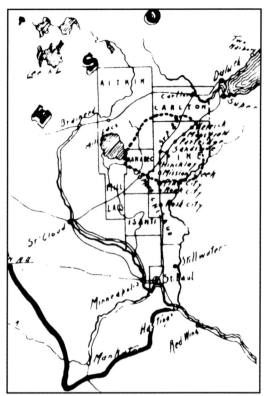

The early morning milk train carried Reverend Anderson north from Hinckley to Sandstone.

has just returned from Hinckley where the air was heavy with the haze and smell of smoke. He'd thought about staying overnight there, but decided to get on the milk train to Sandstone. It left at three o'clock in the morning. Fires stopped the train several times, but Emil hardly noticed.

Emil is still awake the next afternoon, writing a sermon. When he looks out his second-story window, he sees that the sky has turned an eerie red. He later wrote, "All the earth looked as if it had been dipped in blood."

If You Love Your Lives!

Emil flies down the stairs to warn his neighbors on the street. At the telegraph office, a message has come from Hinckley. "If you love your lives," it reads, "try to save them!"

Emil begs people to flee to the river with him. Some do. Others cannot believe they are in danger. Some at the train station even laugh. The water pump operator refuses to leave his post, afraid he will lose his job if he abandons the pump.

Emil bangs on the doors of all the houses along the way to the river. He shouts for everyone to run for their lives. All of a sudden, he catches sight of actual flames. They reach so high that they make the land, the forest, and the buildings look like miniatures.

Suddenly, before the fire hits, a wind rushes in, as hot as a bake oven and as fast as a locomotive. Next, huge fireballs arrive, shooting overhead, coming to within 20 feet of the ground before exploding and sending down a storm of flaming rockets and blinding lights. In the next flash, the fire reaches Sandstone.

Why the Railroads Hired Water Pumpers

Trains used to run on steam. Coal was shoveled into an onboard furnace that boiled water flowing in from a tank car. Trains had to make regular stops at trackside tanks to fill up on water. If the water pumper left his post, a train might get stranded without power, causing catastrophic accidents.

Neighborly Calls

Emil races on, pushed by the hurricane force winds. He comes upon another house. Bursting through the door, he shouts for the three families there to run for the river.

Everyone scrambles out, but in the confusion and terror, one man has forgotten to wait for his wife and 6-month-old baby. Clutching her baby, the wife stumbles outside. The terrific noise and whirling colors, the exploding fireworks and whipping wind confuse her.

Suddenly a gust of scorching wind lifts the mother and child, carrying them about 30 feet and dropping them in a cornfield. Emil hasn't seen this. He's been holding onto the other side of the house to keep from being sucked up into the cyclone.

Sprinting again, Emil hears a cry from the fields. There he finds the mother, too frightened to move. He begs her to let him take the baby, promising to save him if he can save himself. He encourages the mother, telling her to get up and run for the river as fast as she can.

Locked in!

Beyond the cornstalks, the families' little house has already caught fire. Emil clutches the baby and dashes with all his might. When he feels another gust building up beneath them, Emil ducks behind another house. He watches as the baby's house gets lifted and carried away by the firestorm, disintegrating into ashes.

The fire is closing in around them. Emil folds the baby deeper under his shirt. As he darts downhill toward the river, they come upon another house. The kitchen back door is open, but when Emil runs in and screams, no one answers.

Now, the fire is right on top of the house. It meets them at the kitchen door as they try to leave. Emil hugs the baby and dashes through the house to the front door. Locked! He forces it down, but he's lost valuable seconds.

Tornado Winds

As soon as Emil and the baby get out into the street, they find themselves in a great, heaving gust from the firestorm. The hot wind lifts them right off the street and carries them, whistling in their ears. Emil's hair stands on end, and his legs work uselessly, running midair.

When they land, Emil is amazed to find that neither he nor the child is hurt. The storm has carried them down to the river, about a thousand feet away from the front door of that last house!

Jump in!

Through the smoke they see many of their neighbors standing on the banks, about to throw themselves in. A few people are already in the water, covered to their chins. The river is a black mirror reflecting live, red ripples. The scorching air burns down into everyone's lungs and stings their eyes.

In the superheated wind, Emil's clothes burst into flames even though the fire hasn't yet reached him. Clutching the child, he plunges into the water. Suddenly the baby's mother is with them. Emil is glad to give her the baby, safe and sound.

Wet Witnesses

Everyone watches in horror as flames shoot into the sky. The fire is a Niagara of flame, roiling and frothing through the atmosphere. On both banks of the river, haystacks burst into flames like gassed torches. The ripples in the river swell to the size of wind-swept ocean waves.

The fire eats through the walls of the boardinghouses on the riverbanks, poking filigree holes that look like red lace. The people in the river watch as sets of bedroom furniture appear from behind the burned-out walls. These turn a deadly black before exploding into red flames. The burning buildings are then lifted and sucked away.

Everyone in the river hears the awful cries of the "poor perishing people in town who had not heeded the warning." Some had not believed that a forest fire could get so powerful and destroy so quickly.

Most of those who have run for the river in Sandstone are saved. A few die, slipping quietly under the water, overcome by smoke, waves, and terror.

Out of the Woods

When the fuel runs out, the fire dies down. In what used to be forests and towns, for miles around, nothing is left but black char and gray ashes. In many places, the fire has burned everything, down to the subsoil.

Rescue workers set up "relief tents" to care for many needs. In this canvas "town," survivors of the harrowing horror found food, water, medical supplies, and comforting company.

When Peter and Gus come out of the woods and trudge back to Mission Creek, they are shocked. Every house, except one, is gone.

Rescue workers come upon them and tell them of the terrible fire that has destroyed Hinckley and several towns. It has killed hundreds of people. The young men are relieved to learn

Vegetable, Animal, and Mineral

As animals and vegetation die, they form part of the organic matter called "duff" on the forest floor. The same rains which nourish live things then act to disintegrate, or break down, the dead ones. The same sun that helped them grow bakes them brittle. The same air that enlivened them scatters them apart. When a fire is hot enough, this rich soil is burned off until only the underlying mineral dirt remains. In firestorms, even that gets baked. If the soil is clay-based, it will bake to a porcelain-like texture. Sandy soil will melt down to glass.

Where the bustling Hinckley Depot once stood, metal rails are twisted and melted, wooden ties have turned to greasy ash, and all that remains of shade trees are stubs.

21

that their own families are still alive. They survived by lying in the middle of a potato field. Not everyone was as lucky. In some towns, families who had done the very same thing perished.

In Hinckley

In Hinckley, three hundred people scramble aboard a train that races against the fire. When the cars ignite, everyone jumps

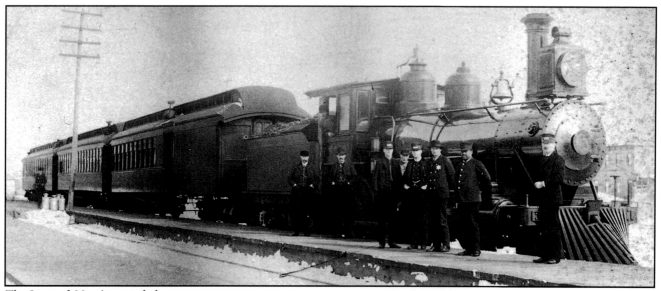

The Limited No. 4 carried three hundred refugees to Skunk Lake, deep in the forest.

out into Skunk Lake to lie in 18 inches of swampy water. The firestorm rages all around for three-quarters of an hour. All are saved, but all are injured by the burning coals and ashes that pelted them.

The burned down area of Skunk Lake after the fire

James Root

The Limited No. 4 train which carried refugees to Skunk Lake was engineered by James Root, who started railroading at the age of 14. During the Civil War, he had driven the train for General Sherman in the decisive March to Atlanta. It was Jim, too, who had carried the first load of liberated Union Soldiers from Andersonville Prison.

John Wesley Blair

Former Slave Helps Save Hundreds

John Wesley Blair, the train porter on the Limited No. 4, was probably born a slave in Arkansas, and freed at age 12 through President Abraham Lincoln's Emancipation Proclamation.

He showed extraordinary virtue, risking his own life for his three hundred charges, most of them Caucasian, or white.

Within six hours, an area of 400 square miles has been laid to waste, burned to the ground, and an estimated six hundred people have perished in the terrible sea of fire. The Great Fire of 1894 has taken men, women, children, and animals. At the water pump in Sandstone, a rescue party finds the faithful operator dead at his post.

It is no easy task breaking through the baked soil of Hinckley to dig graves for the victims.

CHAPTER THREE

The Matheson Fire in Ontario, Canada

Firestorm in Canada

Only 22 years after the Hinckley Fire in Minnesota, the area of northern Ontario, Canada, around the town of Matheson, is also visited by the rare phenomenon of the firestorm.

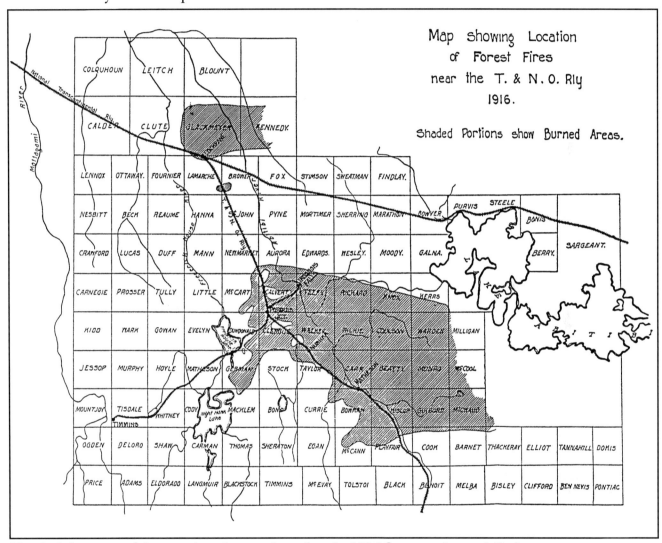

The shaded portions of this map show the areas burned in the 1916 fires in and around Matheson.

The Matheson Fire remains the worst Canadian fire in history, burning 24 townships, 20 of them completely. It claimed at least 243 lives, although the unofficial count is much higher because many of the settlers were isolated and unknown. Ten years before only Native Americans and fur trappers lived in this

After houses, settlers built churches and schools.

The pioneer students and teacher of the first Wah-tay-beaq School, which was destroyed in the 1916 fire

area. Due to the wealth found in Ontario's mineral mines, vast forests, and good soil, it became a "boom area" in 1916, full of fortune seekers and pioneers.

Why Had They Waited?

When this Ontario fire was over, the Lands and Forest Minister and others could not understand why so many lives had

Even though the northern Ontario lands are richly supplied with lakes and rivers, the Matheson Fire of 1916 bore down so quickly that few people had time to take refuge in them.

been lost. After all, it had occurred in an area where people could have taken refuge in the many lakes and rivers.

Those who hadn't experienced the firestorm had no idea that it was not a usual forest fire. It was no wonder they couldn't understand why settlers had waited so long to evacuate. Here's what happened.

The World Is on Fire!

The date is July 29, 1916. Most able-bodied men are across the ocean, fighting World War I. A thick cloud of smoke has been rolling over the area for weeks, and the day before, the temperature reached 100°F (38°C).

In the mid-afternoon hustle and bustle of business-as-usual in Cochrane, a charred farm cart, still smoking, barrels onto the main street. Its horses heave with exhaustion. The farmer stands in his soot-covered clothing, screaming, *"Le monde s'enflamme!"*—"The world's on fire!" His wife and three children in half-burned clothing sit dazed, their eyes big with fear in tiny faces blackened with soot.

How to Boil a Frog

If a frog jumps into boiling water, it will hop right out, but if it sits in water that slowly gets hotter, it will boil to death.

Before the Matheson Fire, the heat in the Ontario region had been increasing so gradually that miners descending below ground were shocked by the chill of the steady 70°F (21°C) temperature there. Those coming up to the surface were collapsing at the entrances to the shafts, flattened by the surprising heat.

27

A Call to Action

People in town run to the train station, hoping for some news. Their normally clear view down the tracks is darkened by heavy smoke, but no one sees fire. Earlier that morning, at 7:10, the station masters at Cochrane and Matheson, 45 miles apart, exchanged telegraph messages. Although both had noticed worsening smoke, neither saw flames. Neither realized that in a little more than eight hours, the world they knew, for a hundred miles around, would be wiped out.

Explosions Without Fires

Kegs of gasoline and oil in the yards of hardware stores begin exploding, their blasts shaking the town. People race to the brick schoolhouse and hospital as fire roars through, scooping up everything in its path.

The blistering air picks up speed, driving the fire southward through the summer forest. In some communities it makes the church bells suddenly peal out, as though ghosts were ringing them.

Making Weather

When the fire blazes into Iroquois Falls, people flee to the brick Abitibi paper mill. A wall of flame, miles wide and sky-high, approaches with an ear-splitting roar. Outside the mill, it

Photo taken at the time of the Matheson Fire

licks up 40,000 chords of wood as if they were hay. Then it cyclones around the building before its winds shift direction, and another firestorm phenomenon occurs. The fire creates its own weather system, wrenching a terrific thunderstorm out of the sky. Thunder booms and lightning blinds. As the fire moves on, much-needed rain pelts down.

Three Short Blasts

Farther south, in Kelso, Dr. Reid is leaving his 12-year-old daughter, Iris, in charge of her younger brothers and sisters while he rushes to help save their school.

A freight train suddenly careens into town, repeatedly sounding three short whistle blasts, the dreaded fire alarm. The train is hissing out bursts of pent-up steam, eager to move on, away from danger. Those who have gotten on in other villages are urging the people from Kelso to jump aboard. Iris has to make a life-and-death decision alone. In the confusion of screaming people and blinding smoke, she hands her siblings up into the waiting hands of other *refugees*, those escaping. Then,

SCHOOL HOUSE
SANDSTONE MINN.

Are Schools Immune from Fire?

In many of the burned-out towns in both Minnesota and Ontario, the only building which remained standing was the school-house. Townspeople built schools from brick, providing children not only with an education, but with the most durable buildings.

her heart pounding, Iris climbs on board, too. When the firestorm bares down on Kelso, the Reid children are far away. But they never see their father again.

In Matheson

At 3:30 in the afternoon, the fire, looking like a strange wall of electric flame, rolls into Matheson. Those who cannot reach the train station leap into the Black River, covering themselves with clothing, potato sacks, and wet blankets. The flames advance like a huge living thing, and people see that the river will not stop it. They scream and duck under water as the sheet of fire roars right over them, seeming to use the very air for fuel. It makes the 300-foot leap over the river and barrels onto the opposite bank.

The death toll is highest where people are cut off from the railroad or a major body of water. For weeks afterwards, rescuers bury Native Americans, lumberjacks, prospectors, and fur trappers who have died in the deep woods.

Each of them supplied with rubber boots, a grave-digging crew pauses in its sorrowful work.

A painting from the period shows how wild animals—prey and predator together—ran for the cover of water.

Strange Riverbed Fellows

Animals of the forest run for their lives, too. A prospector in Ontario staggers toward a creek, stumbling in just as fire reaches him. He hears someone crashing through the woods and leaping into the water. Groping toward his neighbor he cries, "Help me! I can't see!" His hands catch hold of something "very big and hairy." Both he and that moose survive.

Relief Work

In every town, the survivors begin their own relief work, sharing what food they have, tending burns with axle grease from trains, and flushing eyes with river water.

Relief crews bring tents, food, clothing, and medical supplies. The settlers are especially grateful for the hundreds of pairs of rubber boots because what had once been majestic forest is

A family devastated by the fire

31

With all the buildings burned to ashes, survivors gather in a tent town where only the skeletal centers of once-mighty trees remain.

Relief crews brought pine coffins, too, so that those who perished in the fire could have decent burials.

Except for the cast-iron stove on which his granddaughter Flossie stands, nothing remains of Jerry Duggan's home. Everything made of wood, fabric, and paper has disappeared. The metal, glass, and porcelain objects have been melted out of shape.

now a sooty prairie. The 6 to 12 inches of *humus*, rich topsoil, has burned down to the clay subsoil, and in some places, it is baked to a glass-like coating.

Farm animals accompany a refugee couple leaving the stricken area on foot.

Rebuilding

Soon after, people in almost all communities come back to rebuild. A forest fire of that magnitude has never burned there again.

What Do Survivors Eat?

While they wait for relief crews from neighboring towns and cities, survivors of the fires dig up potatoes that have been baked to perfection in the ground. Cows, eager for human company, trot toward them, to be milked.

One family finds only their stove standing. The mother opens the door. The raw loaves she had placed inside have been baked by the fire. They break this bread, sharing it with grateful neighbors.

CHAPTER FOUR

Nature Gets the Last Word

The Forestry Services

Largely because of these two North American disasters, the Forest Services in both the United States and Canada organized ways to stop fires from starting, and once started, from spreading. They controlled fires for many years.

A line of Canadian bush firefighters creating a firebreak with a handheld tool, the Pulaski (a combination ax and hoe)

One of the members of this crew in the 1940's keeps his eye on the course of the smoke, his ax at the ready.

In recent years, however, this old policy has changed. Scientists now know that some fire is good for the forest. It is nature's way of cleaning up and of preventing firestorms from occurring.

After almost one hundred years of controlling fires, the United States Forest Service found in Yellowstone National Park that big fires occur and run wild because little ones are *extinguished*, put out, too soon. If those smaller fires had been allowed to run their courses, they probably would have cleared away the very debris that can cause the uncontrollable firestorms.

In the 1950's, a mother and her children watch as a forest fire is extinguished.

Nature Has the Last Word

At Yellowstone, in 1988, it is not only the months of brave efforts from thousands of firefighters that has stopped the fires. It is the rain and snow that nature brought once autumn came back to the park.

The sun sets on a landscape scarred by fire, refreshed by snow, and ready to rebuild itself in the spring.

Scars Only

Victims of fire rebuild their homes and their lives. Nature rebuilds itself. In Yellowstone, new stands of lodgepole pines are forming. Small animals are making their nests in the short vegetation. The hawks are getting fat. One day, except for the

In a base of sooty black soil, made mineral-rich by fire, new green growth makes its first appearance.

scars, there will hardly be a sign that fire has been to Yellowstone at all. People picnicking on the split boulders may wonder what in the world could have happened to make huge rocks open up like that.

Telling the Future

When and where will a forest fire strike next? No one knows for sure. But scientists and fire managers in both the United States and Canada today are doing their best to decide when to step in and when to let a fire burn. They want to let nature claim what it needs to, but they will fight for human life and property every time it is threatened.

It's a "lucky" day when firefighters in the wild can drive their well-equipped trucks directly to the scene of a blaze!

They are there, watching every small flare-up. At the first sign of danger, they rush to warn people. They use all their knowledge and tools to protect people, animals, and towns. They help everyone leave safely and calmly, with plenty of time to spare. They resolve that no one will ever again have to hear an awful cry like, "Forest fire! Run for your life!"

Index

A

Abitibi: 28
Anderson, Emil: 17–20
Andersonville Prison: 23
animals: 4, 5, 14, 17, 21, 24, 31, 33, 36
Arkansas: 23

B

backburn: 8–9
Black River: 30
Blair, John Wesley: 23

C

Canada: 5, 15, 25–33, 34, 37
Canadian Forest Service: 5
Civil War: 23
Cochrane: 27–28
crown, crowning: 2, 6

D

diversity: 4, 14
drought: 6, 16
duff: 21

E

Emancipation Proclamation: 23

F

fire lines: 7, 8, 9
fire winds: 6, 9
fireballs: 18
firebrands: 6
firestorm: 10, 22, 25, 35

G

General Sherman: 23

Great Fire of 1894: 16–24
ground fires: 2

H

Hinckley: 5, 15–24
Hot Shots: 7, 9
humus: 33

I

Industrial Revolution: 16
Iroquois Falls: 28

J

Johnson, Gus: 17, 21

K

Kelso: 29, 30

L

Limited No. 4: 22, 23
Lincoln, Abraham: 23
locomotives: 16
Lodgepole: 3, 36

M

maps: 18, 25
March to Atlanta: 23
Matheson: 5, 15, 25–33
Minnesota: 5, 15, 16–24
Mission Creek: 17, 21

N

Native Americans: 25, 30
Nyberg, Peter: 17, 21

O

Ontario: 5, 25–33

Continued from previous page

P

phloem: 8
prescribed burn: 8

R

railroad: 16, 18, 21, 22, 23, 29, 30
rangers: 2–7, 37–38
Reid, Dr.: 29
Reid, Iris: 29, 30
relief work: 24, 31–33
rescue workers: 21–24, 30
resin: 3
Root, James: 23

S

Sandstone: 17–21, 24, 29
satellites: 15
schools: 26, 29

Skunk Lake: 22, 23
slurry: 10, 11, 12
smoke jumpers: 11
subsoil: 21
surface fires: 2
survivors: 13, 20, 21, 22, 31, 32, 33, 36

T

technology: 10–13, 15

U

U.S. Forest Service: 5, 34

W

World War I: 15, 27

Y

Yellowstone: 1–14, 34–37

Acknowledgments

The author gratefully acknowledges Brian J. Stocks, Senior Forest Fire Research Scientist, for his generous assistance in supplying critical materials for the text. She also wishes to thank Jeanne Coffey, curator of the Hinckley Fire Museum, who answered the alarm for help, and Laura Rust, Minnesota researcher extraordinaire.

In gathering photo research, many individuals from various organizations made this project their own, and are here cited, with deep gratitude:

Theresa Brownwright, Canadian Bushplane Heritage Centre

Janelle Smith, United States Department of the Interior, Bureau of Land Management, Office of Fire and Aviation

Dianne J. Bush, Thelma Miles Museum

Christine Bourolias, Archives of Ontario

Steve Nielsen, Minnesota Historical Society

Wendy Glassmire, National Geographic Society

And the following, for helpful leads:

Doug Woods, Ontario Department of Lands and Forests; Bob Thomas, Information Officer for Fires; the staffs of the National Archives of Canada and the United States National Park Service

Photo Credits

National Interagency Fire Center
Contents page, p. 1 top, bottom, p. 2 top, p. 3 bottom, p. 4 top, bottom, p. 5 top, bottom, p. 6 bottom, p. 7 top, bottom, p. 8 top, bottom, p. 9 top, bottom, p. 10 top, bottom, p. 12, p. 13, p. 14, p. 15, p. 36 bottom, p. 37

Michael Quinton / NGS Image Collection: p. 3 top
Raymond Gehman / NGS Image Collection: p. 6 top
Richard Olsenius / NGS Image Collection: p. 36 top

Canadian Bushplane Heritage Centre
Cover, Title page, p. 2 bottom, p. 11, p. 19, p. 20, p. 27, p. 34 left, right; p. 35

Minnesota Historical Society
p. 16, p. 17 top, p. 21 top, p. 22 top, p. 29, p. 31 top

Hinckley Fire Museum
p. 17 bottom, p. 18, p. 21 bottom, p. 22 bottom, p. 23 top, bottom, p. 24

National Archives of Canada / C46727: p. 30
National Archives of Canada: p. 31 bottom
National Archives of Canada / C46725: p. 32 middle
National Archives of Canada / C46726: p. 32 bottom

Thelma Miles Museum, Matheson, Ontario
p. 25, p. 26 top, bottom, p. 28, p. 32 top, p. 33

CELEBRA LA LIBERTAD

Canciones, símbolos y frases célebres de los Estados Unidos

Contenido

Canciones	2-9
Símbolos	10-21
Frases célebres	22-31

W9-CGS-178

PEARSON
Scott Foresman

ISBN: 0-328-03696-X

Copyright © 2003, Pearson Education, Inc.

All Rights Reserved. Printed in the United States of America. This publication is protected by Copyright, and permission should be obtained from the publisher prior to any prohibited reproduction, storage in a retrieval system, or transmission in any form by any means, electronic, mechanical, photocopying, recording, or likewise. For information regarding permission(s), write to: Permissions Department, Scott Foresman, 1900 East Lake Avenue, Glenview, Illinois 60025.

5 6 7 8 9 10 V055 11 10 09 08 07 06 05 04 03

Oficinas editoriales: Glenview, Illinois • Parsippany, Nueva Jersey • Nueva York, Nueva York

Oficinas de ventas: Parsippany, Nueva Jersey • Duluth, Georgia • Glenview, Illinois • Coppell, Texas • Ontario, California

www.estudiossocialessf.com

Éste es el himno de los Estados Unidos de América y se canta en inglés.

The Star-Spangled Banner

Escrito por Francis Scott Key

Oh, say! can you see, by the dawn's early light,
What so proudly we hailed at the twilight's last gleaming,
Whose broad stripes and bright stars, through the perilous fight,
O'er the ramparts we watched were so gallantly streaming?
And the rockets' red glare, the bombs bursting in air,
Gave proof through the night that our flag was still there.
Oh, say, does that Star-Spangled Banner yet wave
O'er the land of the free and the home of the brave?

America

**Escrita por
Samuel Francis Smith**

Canción escrita para una celebración del 4 de Julio. Se canta en inglés.

My country! 'tis of thee, Sweet land of liberty, Of thee I sing;
Land where my fathers died, Land of the Pilgrims' pride,
From ev'ry mountainside Let freedom ring!

We the People

5

Canción sobre el paisaje de nuestro país. Se canta en inglés.

America, the Beautiful

Escrita por Katharine Lee Bates
Compuesta por Samuel A. Ward

O beautiful for spacious skies,
For amber waves of grain,
For purple mountain majesties
Above the fruited plain!

America! America!
God shed His grace on thee,
And crown thy good with brotherhood
From sea to shining sea!

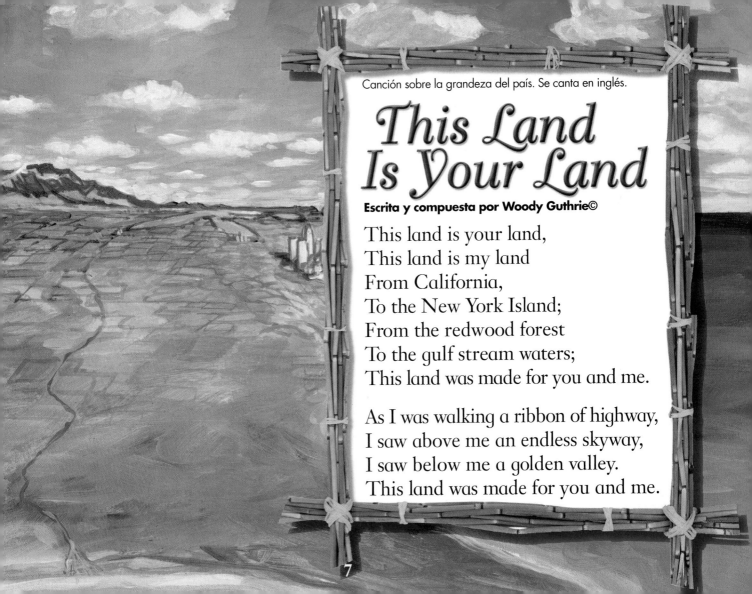

Canción sobre la grandeza del país. Se canta en inglés.

This Land Is Your Land

Escrita y compuesta por Woody Guthrie©

This land is your land,
This land is my land
From California,
To the New York Island;
From the redwood forest
To the gulf stream waters;
This land was made for you and me.

As I was walking a ribbon of highway,
I saw above me an endless skyway,
I saw below me a golden valley.
This land was made for you and me.

Canción popular de la
Guerra de Independencia.
Se canta en inglés.

Yankee Doodle

Escrita por Dr. Richard Shuckburgh

Yankee Doodle went to town,
A-riding on a pony,
Stuck a feather in his hat
And called it macaroni.

Yankee Doodle, keep it up,
Yankee Doodle dandy,
Mind the music and the step
And with the girls be handy.

8

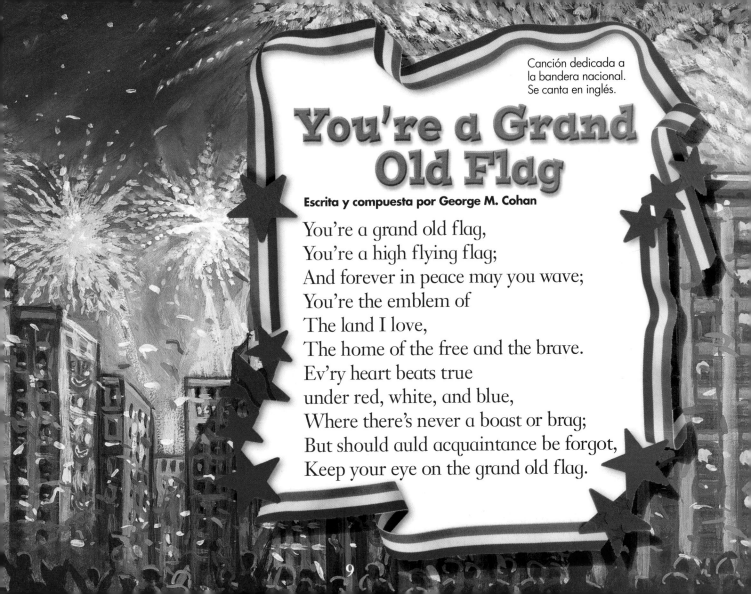

Canción dedicada a
la bandera nacional.
Se canta en inglés.

You're a Grand Old Flag

Escrita y compuesta por George M. Cohan

You're a grand old flag,
You're a high flying flag;
And forever in peace may you wave;
You're the emblem of
The land I love,
The home of the free and the brave.
Ev'ry heart beats true
under red, white, and blue,
Where there's never a boast or brag;
But should auld acquaintance be forgot,
Keep your eye on the grand old flag.

Historia de la bandera

La primera bandera de los Estados Unidos tenía 13 franjas y 13 estrellas, para representar los 13 estados que tenía nuestro país cuando obtuvo la libertad. La bandera de hoy todavía tiene 13 franjas.

La bandera de los Estados Unidos

La bandera de los Estados Unidos es un símbolo de nuestro país. Representa el pueblo, la tierra y la libertad de los Estados Unidos. La bandera ha cambiado con el tiempo.

A nuestra bandera también se le llama Old Glory (Gloria del pasado), Stars and Stripes (Estrellas y Franjas) y Star-Spangled Banner (Bandera estrellada).

En la bandera de los Estados Unidos, el rojo representa la valentía, el blanco representa la bondad y el azul representa la justicia.

¿Lo sabías? La bandera de los Estados Unidos más grande que existe alcanza a cubrir tres campos de futbol americano. Cada estrella es más alta que un autobús escolar.

Honrar la bandera

Debemos izar la bandera con rápidez y bajarla despacio. La bandera nunca debe tocar el suelo.

La bandera no se debe izar cuando el mal tiempo pueda dañarla.

No debemos colocar ninguna otra bandera por encima de la bandera de los Estados Unidos de América.

Mostrar respeto a la bandera

Cuando recites el Juramento a la bandera, debes estar de pie, mirar de frente a la bandera y ponerte la mano derecha sobre el corazón. Cuando cantes o escuches el himno nacional párate y presta atención. Cuando la bandera pase en un desfile, párate y ponte la mano derecha sobre el corazón.

Exhibir la bandera

En general la bandera sólo debe exhibirse del amanecer al atardecer. La bandera se puede exhibir después de que oscurezca si está bien iluminada.

Símbolos nacionales

El águila de cabeza blanca

El águila de cabeza blanca fue escogida como el ave nacional de los Estados Unidos en 1782.

¿Lo sabías? *El águila de cabeza blanca es un ave grande de color café oscuro con plumas blancas en la cabeza y la cola.*

El Tío Sam

El Tío Sam represen el gobierno y el espíri de los Estados Unido

El Tío Sam va vestido con los colores de la bandera de los Estados Unidos.

14

La Campana de la Libertad

La Campana de la Libertad es un símbolo de la libertad de los Estados Unidos. La Campana de la Libertad está en Filadelfia, Pennsylvania.

"Proclamad la libertad por toda la tierra hasta llegar a todos sus habitantes".

En 1846, se tocó la Campana de la Libertad para celebrar el cumpleaños de George Washington. Pero la grieta de la campana se agrandó tanto, que no se volvió a tocar.

El lema de los Estados Unidos

El lema de nuestro país es "En Dios confiamos".

15

Sitios notables de la nación

La Estatua de la Libertad

La Estatua de la Libertad está en la bahía de Nueva York, de frente al mar para dar la bienvenida a quienes llegan a los Estados Unidos de América.

La antorcha ilumina el camino a la libertad y da esperanza a quienes llegan a los Estados Unidos.

La corona tiene siete puntas parecidas a los rayos del sol. Estas puntas representan la luz de la libertad brillando sobre los siete continentes y los siete océanos.

En la tablilla está escrita la fecha de la Declaración de Independencia: 4 de julio de 1776.

¿Lo sabías? *La Estatua de la Libertad mide 152 pies de alto. Es una de las estatuas más grandes del mundo. Muchos visitantes suben los 354 escalones que hay hasta la corona.*

Dentro del monumento se pueden leer dos discursos de Lincoln: el discurso de toma de posesión de su segundo mandato y el Discurso de Gettysburg.

Las banderas que rodean el Monumento a Washington representan los 50 estados.

El Monumento a Lincoln

El Monumento a Lincoln honra a Abraham Lincoln, el presidente número 16 de los Estados Unidos.

El Monumento a Washington

El Monumento a Washington, en honor a George Washington, es más alto que cualquier otra edificación en Washington, D.C.

La Estatua de la Libertad que está en la punta del Capitolio mide casi 20 pies de alto.

El Capitolio de los Estados Unidos

El Capitolio de los Estados Unidos, ubicado en Washington, D.C., es donde se reúne el Congreso.

El Capitolio también es un museo. Tiene muchas pinturas y estatuas de personajes y líderes importantes.

¿*Lo sabías?* *El Capitolio tiene unas 540 salas. En todo el edificio hay más o menos 850 puertas.*

La Corte Suprema de Justicia

La Corte Suprema se reúne en el edificio de la Corte Suprema de Justicia desde 1935.

Encima de la puerta principal del edificio hay una inscripción con el lema: "Igualdad ante la ley".

La Casa Blanca

La Casa Blanca es la casa del presidente de los Estados Unidos. George Washington fue el único presidente que nunca vivió allí.

Durante muchos años, el río Colorado
talló capas de roca para formar el cañón.

En el parque viven cabras, osos,
alces y muchos otros animales.

El Gran Cañón

El Gran Cañón de Arizona tiene cerca
de 277 millas de largo y una milla de
profundidad. En algunos sitios, tiene
casi 18 millas de ancho.

Parque Nacional de los Glaciare

En el Parque Nacional de los Glaciares, ubicad
en Montana, hay más de 50 glaciares, o grandes
bloques de hielo. El parque es famoso por sus
bellas montañas.

Algunos pastos de llanura llegan
a medir 10 pies de alto.

Algunos cipreses tienen casi
700 años.

Reserva Tallgrass Prairie

Más de 40 variedades de pasto crecen en
esta reserva de praderas de pastizales,
ubicada en Kansas.

Reserva Nacional Big Cypress

El pantano "Big Cypress" es el hogar de una
gran variedad de plantas y animales. Panteras
de la Florida, caimanes, nutrias y muchas
clases de aves viven aquí.

Juramento a la bandera

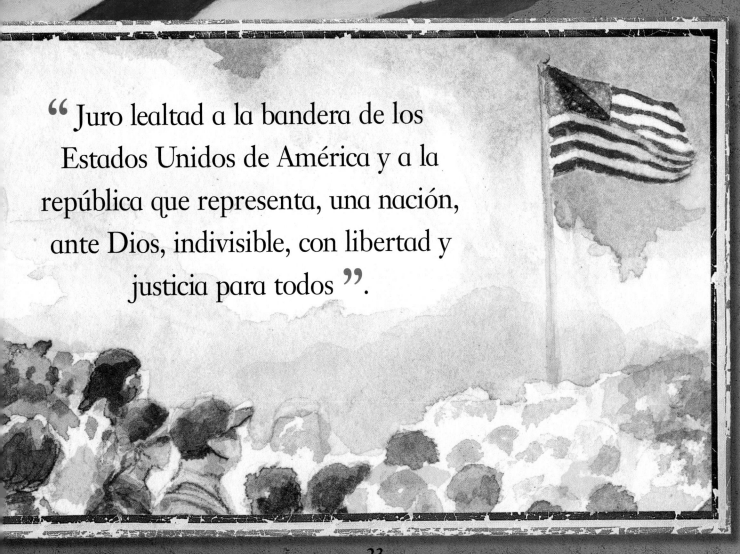

" Juro lealtad a la bandera de los Estados Unidos de América y a la república que representa, una nación, ante Dios, indivisible, con libertad y justicia para todos ".

Palabras de libertad

"Sostenemos como verdades evidentes que todos los hombres nacen iguales, que están dotados por el Creador de ciertos derechos inalienables, entre los cuales se cuentan el derecho a la Vida, a la Libertad y a la búsqueda de la Felicidad".

Declaración de Independencia

"Nosotros, el pueblo de los Estados Unidos, con el fin de hacer más perfecta la Unión, establecer la justicia, asegurar la tranquilidad nacional, proveer a la defensa común, fomentar el bienestar genera y afianzar los beneficios de libertad para nosotros mismos y para nuestros descendientes, decretamo e instituimos esta Constitución para los Estados Unidos de América".

Preámbulo a la Constitución

"...un gobierno del pueblo, por el pueblo y para el pueblo no desaparecerá de la Tierra".
Abraham Lincoln

"El mundo debe hacerse seguro para la democracia".
Woodrow Wilson

"Dadme vuestras masas cansadas, pobres y apiñadas, ansiosas de respirar libres, los infelices despojos de vuestra atestada playa. Enviad a los desamparados arrojados por la tempestad. Yo levanto mi lámpara al lado de la puerta dorada".
Emma Lazarus

"Tengo el sueño de que mis cuatro hijos algún día vivan en una nación donde no sean juzgados por el color de su piel sino por el contenido de su carácter".
Dr. Martin Luther King, Jr.

"Es enteramente cierto que un gobierno popular no puede florecer sin la virtud de su pueblo".
Richard Henry Lee, firmante de la Declaración de Independencia

Bondad

" ... lo más importante en cualquier relación no es lo que recibas sino lo que des ".

Eleanor Roosevelt

" Los más felices son los que hacen más por los demás ".

Booker T. Washington

" Creo que... toda mente humana siente placer al hacer el bien a los demás ".

Thomas Jefferson

" Sin malicia hacia nadie; con caridad hacia todos... ".

Abraham Lincoln

" Ningún acto de amabilidad, por pequeño que sea, se malgastará ".

Esopo

" Si logras que tu corazón se preocupe por alguien más, habrás triunfado ".

Dra. Maya Angelou, poeta

" Nunca pierdas la oportunidad de decir una palabra amable ".

William Makepeace Thackeray, escritor

Respeto

"La mayoría del pueblo estadounidense aún cree que cada individuo de este país tiene derecho al mismo respeto, a la misma dignidad, que cualquier otro individuo".

Barbara Jordan,
congresista de los Estados Unidos, 1973–1979

"Es responsabilidad de todos los ciudadanos de todos los sectores de este país respetar los derechos de los demás…".

John F. Kennedy

"Debemos respetar a los demás como nos respetamos a nosotros mismos".

U Thant, secretario general de las
Naciones Unidas, 1961–1971

"Ansío aprender de los demás. Mi padre creía que uno podía aprender de… un granjero o de un presidente… y debemos respetar a ambos por igual".

Dra. Blandina Cárdenas, educadora

"… se puede decir de nuestra nación: que garantizamos el respeto a la ley y un tratamiento equitativo ante la ley, para débiles y poderosos, para ricos y pobres…".

James Earl (Jimmy) Carter

27

Responsabilidad

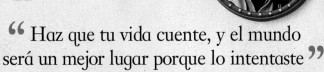

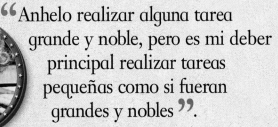

"Anhelo realizar alguna tarea grande y noble, pero es mi deber principal realizar tareas pequeñas como si fueran grandes y nobles".

Helen Keller

"Mis queridos compatriotas: no se pregunten qué puede hacer su país por ustedes, sino qué pueden hacer ustedes por su país".

John F. Kennedy

"Debemos emplear nuestra vida en hacer que el mundo sea un mejor lugar…".

Dolores Huerta, líder sindical

"Haz que tu vida cuente, y el mundo será un mejor lugar porque lo intentaste".

Ellison Onizuka, astronauta

"Da lo mejor de ti en cada tarea que realices, no importa cuán insignificante parezca ser en ese momento".

Sandra Day O'Connor

"Sea cual sea el trabajo que realices en la vida, hazlo bien".

Dr. Martin Luther King, Jr.

"Los Estados Unidos en su mejor expresión son un lugar donde la responsabilidad personal se valora y se da por sentada".

George W. Bush

Justicia

" Me gustaría que se me conociera como una persona que se preocupa por la libertad, la igualdad, la justicia y la prosperidad para todos ".

Rosa Parks

" La libertad y la dignidad del individuo se han ofrecido y protegido aquí más que en cualquier otro lugar de la Tierra ".

Ronald Reagan

" Hace ochenta y siete años nuestros padres forjaron en este continente una nueva nación, ideada en libertad y consagrada a la premisa de que todos los hombres son creados iguales ".

Abraham Lincoln

" La Constitución de los Estados Unidos no reconoce distinción alguna entre los ciudadanos por razón de color ".

Frederick Douglass

" ...sin igualdad no puede haber democracia ".

Eleanor Roosevelt

" No puede haber un principio más verdadero que éste: que cada individuo de la comunidad en general tiene el mismo derecho a la protección del gobierno ".

Alexander Hamilton

Honestidad

"La honestidad es el primer capítulo del libro de la sabiduría".

Thomas Jefferson

"No hay que decir muchas palabras para decir la verdad".

Jefe Joseph, líder nez percé

"Regala la verdad y te será retribuida del mismo modo".

Madeline Bridges, poeta

"Nunca te encontrarás a ti mismo hasta que digas la verdad".

Pearl Bailey, actriz y escritora

"La vida de la nación está asegurada siempre y cuando la nación sea honesta, veraz y virtuosa".

Frederick Douglass

"Confío en poseer siempre la firmeza y la virtud suficientes para mantener lo que considero es el más envidiable de los títulos: el carácter de un hombre honesto".

George Washington

"No hay nada más poderoso que la verdad".

Daniel Webster

30

Valentía

"Sólo tú pones límites a lo que puedes lograr. No temas alcanzar las estrellas".

Dra. Ellen Ochoa, astronauta

"El momento de hacer lo correcto siempre es el correcto".

Dr. Martin Luther King, Jr.

"La valentía es la primera de las cualidades humanas porque es la cualidad que garantiza todas las demás".

Winston Churchill

"El defender lo correcto cuando se trata de algo que no tiene aceptación, es una verdadera prueba del carácter moral".

*Margaret Chase Smith,
congresista de los Estados Unidos, 1940–1972*

"Sin valentía, no podemos practicar ninguna otra virtud con firmeza. No podemos ser amables, sinceros, compasivos, generosos ni honestos".

Dra. Maya Angelou, poeta

"Se necesita tanto valor para intentarlo y fracasar como para intentarlo y triunfar".

Anne Morrow Lindbergh, Writer

Reconocimientos

Illustrations
2,3 Marc Scott; 4,5 Robert Gunn; 6,7 Tom Foty; 8,9 Anthony Carnabuci; 10, 11 Cheryl Kirk Noll; 22, 23 Holly Flagg

Songs
THIS LAND IS YOUR LAND, Words and Music by Woody Guthrie. TRO — © Copyright 1956 (Renewed) 1958 (Renewed) 1970 (Renewed) Ludlow Music, Inc., New York, NY. Used by Permission.
"Yankee Doodle," Words by Dr. Richard Shuckburgh from THE MUSIC CONNECTION, Gr. 2 by Jane Beethoven et al., p. 199. Copyright © 2000 by Silver Burdett Ginn Inc. Reprinted by permission of Pearson Education, Inc.

Photographs
Every effort has been made to secure permission and provide appropriate credit for photographic material. The publisher deeply regrets any omission and pledges to correct errors called to their attention in subsequent editions. Unless otherwise acknowledged, all photographs are the property of Scott Foresman, a division of Pearson Education.

12 Siede Preis/PhotoDisc; 13 PhotoDisc; 14 (TC) © Grant V. Faint/Getty Images/The Image Bank, (BR) Obverse ©, (BL) W. Perry Conway/Corbis; 15 (C) © Leif Skoogfors/Corbis-Bettmann; 16 (C) © Bill Ross/Corbis; 17 (TL) © Bettmann/Corbis, (TR) James P. Blair/PhotoDisc; 18 (C) SuperStock; 19 (TL) SuperStock, (BL) Jeremy Woodhouse/PhotoDisc; 20 (TL) © Danny Lehman/Corbis, (TR) © Jon Eisberg/Getty Images/FPG; 21 (TR) Alan and Sandy Carey/PhotoDisc, (TC) © Gary Randall/Unicorn Stock Photos; 24 (B) The Granger Collection, New York; 25 (TC, TR, BR) Library of Congress, (CL) © Bettmann/Corbis; 26 (TL, TR) Library of Congress, (BL) © Mitchell Gerber/Corbis; 27 (TL) United States Senate, (TR, BC) © Bettmann/Corbis; 28 (TL) © Bettmann/ Corbis, (TR) NASA, (BL) Corbis, (BC) © AFP/Corbis; 29 (TL) © Reuters NewMedia Inc./Corbis, (BR) © Archivo Iconográfico, S. A./Corbis; 30 (TL, TR) Library of Congress, (BL, BR) © Bettmann/Corbis; 31 (TL) NASA, (TR) Library of Congress, (BL, BR) © Bettmann/Corbis